THE SHANTY BOOK, SAILOR SHANTIES • VOLUME I • TERRY, RICHARD RUNCIMAN

PAGE
FOREWORD 1
by Sir Walter Runciman iii 1
INTRODUCTION 2
v.. 2
NOTES ON THE SHANTIES............ 7
xiii 7

WINDLASS & CAPSTAN SHANTIES:

1 Billy Boy 10 210
2 Bound for the Rio Grande 11 411
3 Good-bye, fare ye well............ 11 611
4 Johnny come down to Hilo 12 812
5 Clear the track, let the Bullgine run 12
10.. 12
6 Lowlands away 13 1213
7 Sally Brown 13 1613
8 Santy Anna............................. 14 1814
9 Shenandoah 14 2014
10 Stormalong John 14 2214
11 The Hog's-eye Man 15 2415
12 The Wild Goose Shanty 15 2615
13 We're all bound to go 16 2816
14 What shall we do with the drunken sailor? 16 3016

HALLIARD SHANTIES:

15 Blow, my bully boys 17 3217
16 Blow the man down 17 3417
17 Cheer'ly, men....................... 18 3617
18 Good morning, ladies all...... 18 3818
19 Hanging Johnny 18 4018
20 Hilo Somebody 18 4218
21 Oh run, let the Bullgine run 19 4419
22 Reuben Ranzo 19 4619
23 The Dead Horse 20 4820
24 Tom's gone to Hilo 20 5020
25 Whisky Johnny..................... 20 5220
26 Boney was a warrior 20 5420

FORE-SHEET OR SWEATING-UP SHANTIES:

27 Johnny Boker 21 5521
28 Haul away, Joe 21 5621
29 We'll haul the bowlin' 22 5822

BUNT SHANTY:

30 Paddy Doyle's boots 22 5922

ALPHABETICAL INDEX OF SHANTIES

PAGE
Billy Boy...................................... 10 210
Blow, my bully boys 17 3217
Blow the man down 17 3417
Boney was a warrior 20 5420
Bound for the Rio Grande.......... 11 411
Cheer'ly, men............................. 18 3617
Clear the track, let the Bullgine run .. 12 10.. 12
Dead Horse, The 20 4820
Good-bye, fare ye well............... 11 611
Good morning, ladies all........... 18 3818
Hanging Johnny 18 4018
Haul away, Joe 21 5621
Hilo Somebody 18 4218
Hog's-eye Man, The 15 2415
Johnny Boker 21 5521
Johnny come down to Hilo 12 812
Lowlands away 13 1213
Oh run, let the Bullgine run 19 4419
Paddy Doyle's boots 22 5922
Reuben Ranzo 19 4619
Sally Brown 13 1613
Santy Anna................................ 14 1814
Shenandoah 14 2014
Stormalong John 14 2214
Tom's gone to Hilo 20 5020
We'll haul the bowlin' 22 5822
We're all bound to go............... 16 2816
What shall we do with the drunken sailor?.. 16 3016
Whisky Johnny.......................... 20 5220
Wild Goose Shanty, The 15 2615

Publisher's Note

Purchase of this book entitles you to a free trial membership in the publisher's book club at www.rarebooksclub.com. (Time limited offer.) Simply enter the barcode number from the back cover onto the membership form on our home page. The book club entitles you to select from millions of books at no additional charge. You can also download a digital copy of this and related books to read on the go. Simply enter the title or subject onto the search form to find them.

Note: This is an historic book. Pages numbers, where present in the text, refer to the first edition of the book and may also be in indexes.

If you have any questions, could you please be so kind as to consult our Frequently Asked Questions page at www.rarebooksclub.com/faqs.cfm? You are also welcome to contact us there.
Publisher: General Books LLC™, Memphis, TN, USA, 2012. ISBN: 9781153756648.
Proofreading: pgdp.net

❧ ❧ ❧ ❧ ❧ ❧ ❧ ❧

The Shanty Book

Part I

Sailor Shanties

(Curwen Edition 6308)

Collected and Edited, with Pianoforte Accompaniment, by RICHARD RUNCIMAN TERRY, with a Foreword by SIR WALTER RUNCIMAN, Bart.
LONDON
J. Curwen & Sons Ltd., 24 Berners Street, W. 1
Copyright, 1921, by J. Curwen & Sons Ltd.

[Pg iii]

FOREWORD

By SIR WALTER RUNCIMAN

I T is sometimes difficult for old sailors like myself to realize that these fine shanty tunes—so fascinating to the musician, and which no sailor can hear without emotion—died out with the sailing vessel, and now belong to a chapter of maritime history that is definitely closed. They will never more be heard on the face of the waters, but it is well that they should be preserved with reverent care, as befits a legacy from the generation of seamen that came to an end with the stately vessels they manned with such skill and resource.

In speech, the old-time 'shellback' was notoriously reticent—almost inarticulate; but in song he found self-expression, and all the romance and poetry of the sea are breathed into his shanties, where simple childlike sentimentality alternates with the Rabelaisian humour of the grown man. Whatever landsmen may think about shanty words—with their cheerful inconsequence, or lighthearted coarseness—there can be no two opinions about the tunes, which, as folk-music, are a national asset.

I know, of course, that several shanty collections are in the market, but as a sailor I am bound to say that only one—Capt. W.B. Whall's 'Sea Songs, Ships, and Shanties'—can be regarded as authoritative. Only a portion of Capt. Whall's delightful book is devoted to shanties, of which he prints the melodies only (without accompaniment); and of these he does not profess to give more than those he himself learnt at sea. I am glad, therefore, to welcome Messrs. Curwen's project of a wide and representative collection. Dr. Terry's qualifications as editor are exceptional, since he was reared in an environment of nineteenth-century seamen, and is the only landsman I have met who is able to render shanties as the old seamen did. I am not musician enough to criticize his pianoforte accompaniments, but I can vouch for the authenticity of the *melodies* as he presents them, untampered with in any way.

WALTER RUNCIMAN.
Shoreston Hall,
Chathill, 1921.
[Pg iv]

[Pg v]

INTRODUCTION
APOLOGIA
I T may reasonably be asked by what authority a mere landsman publishes a book on a nautical subject. I may, therefore, plead in extenuation that I have all my life been closely connected with seafaring matters, especially during childhood and youth, and have literally 'grown up with' shanties. My maternal ancestors followed the sea as far back as the family history can be traced, and sailor uncles and grand-uncles have sung shanties to me from my childhood upwards. During boyhood I was constantly about amongst ships, and had learnt at first hand all the popular shanties before any collection of them appeared in print. I have in later years collected them from all manner of sailors, chiefly at Northumbrian sources. I have collated these later versions with those which I learnt at first hand as a boy from sailor relatives, and also aboard ship. And lastly, I lived for some years in the West Indies, one of the few remaining spots where shanties may still be heard, where my chief recreation was cruising round the islands in my little ketch. In addition to hearing them in West Indian seaports, aboard Yankee sailing ships and sugar droghers, I also heard them sung constantly on shore in Antigua under rather curious conditions. West Indian negro shanties are movable wooden huts, and when a family wishes to change its *venue* it does so in the following manner: The shanty is levered up on to a low platform on wheels, to which two very long ropes are attached. The ropes are manned by as many hands as their length will admit. A 'shantyman' mounts the roof of the hut and sits astride it. He sings a song which has a chorus, and is an exact musical parallel of a seaman's 'pull-and-haul' shanty. The crowd below sings the chorus, giving a pull on the rope at the required points in the music, just as sailors did when hauling at sea. Each pull on the rope draws the hut a short distance forward, and the process is continued till its final resting-place is reached, when the shantyman descends from the roof. The hut is then levered off the platform on to *terra firma* and fixed in its required position.

WHAT A SHANTY IS
Shanties were labour songs sung by sailors of the merchant service only while at work, and never by way of recreation. Moreover—at least, in the nineteenth century—they were never used aboard men-o'-war, where all orders were carried out in silence to the pipe of the bo'sun's whistle.

Before the days of factories and machinery, all forms of work were literally *manual* labour, and all the world over the labourer, obeying a primitive instinct, sang at his toil: the harvester with his sickle, the weaver at the loom, the spinner at the wheel. Long after machinery had driven the labour-song from the land it survived at sea in the form of shanties, since all work aboard a sailing vessel was performed by hand.

The advent of screw steamers sounded the death-knell of the shanty. Aboard the steamer there were practically no sails to be manipulated; the donkey-engine and steam winch supplanted the hand-worked windlass and capstan. By the end of the seventies steam had driven the sailing ship from the seas. A number of sailing vessels lingered on through the eighties, but they retained little of the corporate pride and splendour that was once theirs. The old spirit was gone never to return.

When the sailing ship ruled the waters and the shanty was a living thing no one appears to have paid heed to it. To the landsman of those days—before folk-song hunting had begun—the haunting beauty of the tunes would appear to have made no appeal. This may be partly accounted for by the fact that he would never be likely to hear the sailor sing them ashore, and partly because of the Rabelaisian character of the words to which they were sung aboard ship. We had very prim notions of propriety in those days, and were apt to overlook the beauty of the melodies, and to speak of shanties in bulk as 'low vulgar songs.' Be that as it may, it was not until the late eighties—when the shanty was beginning to die out with the sailing ship—that any attempt was made to form a collection.

ORIGIN OF THE WORD

Here let me enter my protest against the literary preciosity which derives the word from (*un*) *chanté* and spells it 'chanty'—in other words, against the gratuitous assumption that unlettered British sailors derived one of the commonest words in their vocabulary from a foreign source. The result of this 'literary' spelling is that ninety-nine landsmen out of every hundred, instead of pronouncing the [Pg vi] word 'shanty,' rhyming with 'scanty' (*as every sailor did*), pronounce it 'tchahnty,' rhyming with 'auntie,' thereby courting the amusement or contempt of every seaman. The vogue of '*ch*anty' was apparently created by the late W.E. Henley, a fine poet, a great man of letters, a profound admirer of shanty tunes, but entirely unacquainted with nautical affairs. Kipling and other landsmen have given additional currency to the spelling. The 'literary' sailors, Clark Russell and Frank Bullen, have also spelt it '*ch*anty,' but their reason is obvious. The modest seaman always bowed before the landsman's presumed superiority in 'book-larnin'.' What more natural than that Russell and Bullen, obsessed by so ancient a tradition, should accept uncritically the landsman's spelling. But educated sailors devoid of 'literary' pretensions have always written the word as it was pronounced. To my mind the strongest argument against the literary landsman's derivation of the word is that the British sailor cultivated the supremest contempt for everything French, and would be the last person to label such a definitely British practice as shanty-singing with a French title. If there had been such a thing in French ships as a labour-song bearing such a far-fetched title as (*un*) *chanté*, there might have been a remote possibility of the British sailor adopting the French term in a spirit of sport or derision, but there is no evidence that any such practice, or any such term, achieved any vogue in French ships. As a matter of fact, the Oxford Dictionary (which prints it '*sh*anty') states that the word never found its way into print until 1869.

The truth is that, however plausible the French derivation theory may sound, it is after all pure speculation—and a landsman's speculation at that—unsupported by a shred of concrete evidence.

If I wished to advance another theory more plausible still, and equally unconvincing, I might urge that the word was derived from the negro hut-removals already mentioned. Here, at least, we have a very ancient custom, which would be familiar to British seamen visiting West Indian seaports. The object moved was a *shanty*; the music accompanying the operation was called, by the negroes, a *shanty* tune; its musical form (solo and chorus) was identical with the sailor *shanty*; the pulls on the rope followed the same method which obtained at sea; the soloist was called a *shantyman*; like the shantyman at sea he did no work, but merely extemporized verses to which the workers at the ropes supplied the chorus; and finally, the negroes still pronounce the word itself exactly as the seaman did.

I am quite aware of the flaws in the above argument, but at least it shows a manual labour act performed both afloat and ashore under precisely similar conditions as to (*a*) its nature, (*b*) its musical setting; called by the same name, *with the same pronunciation* in each case; and lastly, connected, in one case, with an actual hut or *shanty*. Against this concrete argument we have a landsman's abstract speculation, which (*a*) begs the whole question, and (*b*) which was never heard of until a few years before the disappearance of the sailing ship. I do not assert that the negroid derivation is conclusive, but that from (*un*) *chanté* will not bear serious inspection.

BIBLIOGRAPHY

The material under this head is very scanty. Nothing of any consequence was written before the eighties, when W.L. Alden, in *Harper's Magazine*, and James Runciman, in the *St. James's Gazette* and other papers, wrote articles on the subject with musical quotations. Since then several collections have appeared:

1887. *Sailors' Songs or Chanties*, the words by Frederick J. Davis, R.N.R., the music composed and arranged upon traditional sailor airs by Ferris Tozer, Mus. D. Oxon.

1888. *The Music of the Waters*, by Laura Alexandrine Smith.

1910 and 1912. *Sea Songs, Ships, and Shanties*, by Capt. W.B. Whall.

1912. *Songs of Sea Labour*, by Frank T. Bullen and W.F. Arnold.

1914. *English Folk Chanteys* with Pianoforte Accompaniment, collected by Cecil J. Sharp.

Of all these collections Capt. Whall's is the only one which a sailor could accept as authoritative. Capt. Whall unfortunately only gives the twenty-eight shanties which he himself learnt at sea. But to any one who has heard them sung aboard the old sailing ships, his versions ring true, and have a bite and a snap that is lacking in those published by mere collectors.

Davis and Tozer's book has had a great vogue, as it was for many years the only one on the market. But the statement that the music is 'composed and arranged on traditional sailor airs' rules it out of court in the eyes of seamen, since (*a*) a sailor song is not a shanty, and (*b*) to 'compose and arrange on traditional airs' is to destroy the traditional form. [Pg vii]

Miss Smith's book is a thick volume into which was tumbled indiscriminately and uncritically a collection of all sorts of tunes from all sorts of countries which had any connection with seas, lakes, rivers, or their geographical equivalents. Scientific folk-song collecting was not understood in those days, and consequently all was fish that came to the authoress's net. Sailor shanties and landsmen's nautical effusions were jumbled together higgledy-piggledy, along with 'Full Fathom Five' and the 'Eton Boating Song.' But this lack of discrimination, pardonable in those days, was not so serious as the inability to write the tunes down correctly. So long as they were copied from other song-books they were not so bad, but when it came to taking them down from the seamen's singing the results were deplorable. Had the authoress been able to give us correct versions of the shanties her collection would have been a valuable one. The book contains altogether about thirty-two shanties collected from sailors in the Tyne seaports. Since both Miss Smith and myself hail from Newcastle, her 'hunting ground' for shanties was also mine, and I am consequently in a position to assess the importance or unimportance of her work. I may, therefore, say that although hardly a single shanty is noted down correctly, I can see clearly—having myself noted the same tunes in the same district—what she intended to convey, and furthermore can vouch for the accuracy of some of the words which were common to north country sailors, and which have not appeared in other collections.

If I have been obliged to criticize Miss Smith's book it is not because I wish to disparage a well-intentioned effort, but because I constantly hear *The Music of the Waters* quoted as an authoritative work on sailor shanties; and since the shanties in it were all collected in the district where I spent boyhood and youth, I am familiar with all of them, and can state definitely that they are in no sense authoritative. I should like, however, to pay my tribute of respect to Miss Smith's industry, and to her enterprise in calling attention to tunes that then seemed in a fair way to disappear.

Bullen and Arnold's book ought to have been a valuable contribution to shanty literature, as Bullen certainly knew his shanties, and used to sing them capitally. Unfortunately his musical collaborator does not appear to have been gifted with the faculty of taking down authentic versions from his singing. He seems to have had difficulty in differentiating between long measured notes and unmeasured pauses; between the respective meanings of three-four and six-eight time; between modal and modern tunes; and between the cases where irregular barring was or was not required. Apart from the amateur nature of the harmonies, the book exhibits such strange unacquaintance with the rudiments of musical notation as the following (p. 25):

1912. *The Espérance Morris Book*, Part II (Curwen Edition 8571), contains five shanties collected and arranged by Clive Carey.

1914. *Shanties and Forebitters*, collected and accompaniments written by Mrs. Clifford Beckett (Curwen Edition 6293).

Journal of the Folk-Song Society, Nos. 12, 18, and 20, contain articles on shanties, with musical examples (melodies only), which, from the academic point of view, are not without interest.

1920. *The Motherland Song Book* (Vols. III and IV, edited by R. Vaughan Williams) contains seven shanties. It is worthy of note that Dr. Vaughan Williams, Mr. Clive Carey, and Mrs. Clifford Beckett all spell the word 'shanty' as sailors pronounced it.

1920. *Sailor Shanties arranged for Solo and Chorus of Men's Voices* by the present editor; two selections (Curwen Edition 50571 and 50572).

There are one or two other collections in print which are obviously compilations, showing no original research. Of these I make no note.

SHANTY FORMS

Shanties may be roughly divided, as regards their use, into two classes: (*a*) Hauling shanties, and (*b*) Windlass and Capstan. The former class accompanied the setting of the sails, and the latter the weighing of the anchor, or 'warping her in' to the wharf, etc. Capstan shanties were also used for pumping ship. A few shanties were 'interchangeable,' i.e. they were used for both halliards and capstan. The subdivisions of each class are interesting, and the nature of the work involving 'walk away,' 'stamp and go,' 'sweating her up,' 'hand over hand,' and other types of shanty would make [Pg viii] good reading; but nautical details, however fascinating, must be economized in a musical publication.

Capstan shanties are readily distinguishable by their music. The operation of walking round the capstan (pushing the capstan bars in front of them) was continuous and not intermittent. Both tune and chorus were, as a rule, longer than those of the hauling shanty, and there was much greater variety of rhythm. Popular songs, if they had a chorus or refrain, could be, and were, effectively employed for windlass and capstan work.

Hauling shanties were usually shorter than capstan ones, and are of two types: (*a*) those used for 'the long hoist' and (*b*) those required for 'the short pull' or 'sweating-up.' Americans called these operations the 'long' and the 'short drag.' The former was used when beginning to hoist sails, when the gear would naturally be slack and moderately easy to manipulate. It had two short choruses, with a double pull in each. In the following example, the pulls are marked

'What shall we do with the drunken sailor?' No. 14, and 'The Hog's-Eye Man,' No. 11. Others fulfil to a certain extent modal conditions, but are nevertheless in keys, e.g. 'Stormalong John,' No. 10.

Like many other folk-songs, certain shanties—originally, no doubt, in a mode—were, by the insertion of leading notes, converted into the minor key. There was also the tendency on the part of the modern sailor to turn his minor key into a major one. I sometimes find sailors singing in the major, nowadays, tunes which the very old men of my boyhood used to sing in the minor. A case in point is 'Haul away, Joe,' No. 28. Miss Smith is correct in giving it in the minor form which once obtained on the Tyne, and I am inclined to hazard the opinion that that was the original form and not, as now, the following:

'The Drunken Sailor' (a distinctly modal tune) sung in the major as follows: [Pg ix]

'Boney was a warrior,' changing to 'Haul the Bowlin'' for 'sweating-up.' In the enthusiasm of their singing, and the absence of any officer to call ''Vast hauling,' they continued operations until they broke the topsail yard in two, when the sight of the wreckage and the fear of consequences brought the singing to an abrupt conclusion. In my then ignorance I naturally asked: 'Why couldn't you have sung shanties without hoisting the topsail?' and the reply was: 'How could we sing a shanty without having our hands on the rope?' Here we have the whole psychology of the labour-song: the old woman could not keen without the 'body,' and the young apprentices could not sing shanties apart from the work to which they belonged. The only truly satisfactory results which I ever get nowadays from an old sailor are when he has been stimulated by conversation to become reminiscent, and croons his shanties almost subconsciously. Whenever I find a sailor willing to declaim shanties in the style of a song I begin to be a little suspicious of his seamanship. In one of the journals of the Folk-Song Society there is an account of a sailor who formed a little party of seafaring men to give public performances of shanties on the concert platform. No doubt this was an interesting experience for the listeners, but that a self-conscious performance such as this could represent the old shanty singing I find it difficult to believe. Of course I have had sailors sing shanties to me in a fine declamatory manner, but I usually found one of three things to be the case: the man was a 'sea lawyer,' or had not done much deep-sea sailing; or his seamanship only dated from the decline of the sailing vessel.

It is doubtless interesting to the folk-songer to see in print shanties taken down from an individual sailor with his individual melodic twirls and twiddles. But since no two sailors ever sing the same shanty quite in the same manner, there must necessarily be some means of getting at the tune, unhampered by these individual idiosyncrasies, which are quite a different thing from what folk-song students recognize as 'variants.' The power to discriminate can only be acquired by familiarity with the shanty as it was in its palmy days. The collector who comes upon the scene at this late time of day must necessarily be at a disadvantage. The ordinary methods which he would apply to [Pg x] a folk-song break down in the case of a labour-song. Manual actions were the soul of the shanty; eliminate these and you have only the skeleton of what was once a living thing. It is quite possible, I know, to push this line of argument too far, but every one who knows anything about seamanship must feel that a shanty nowadays cannot be other than a pale reflection of what it once was.

That is why I deprecate the spurious authenticity conferred by print upon isolated versions of shanties sung by individual old men. When the originals are available it seems to me pedantic and academic to put into print the comic mispronunciations of well-known words by old and uneducated seamen.

And this brings me to the last difficulty which confronts the collector with no previous knowledge of shanties. As a mere matter of dates, any sailors now remaining from sailing ship days must necessarily be very old men. I have found that their octogenarian memories are not always to be trusted. On one occasion an old man sang quite glibly a tune which was in reality a *pasticcio* of three separate shanties all known to me. I have seen similar results in print, since the collector arrived too late upon the scene to be able to detect the tricks which an old man's memory played him.

One final remark about collectors which has an important bearing upon the value of their work. There were two classes of sailing vessels that sailed from English ports—the coaster or the mere collier that plied between the Tyne or Severn and Boulogne, and the Southspainer, under which term was comprised all deep-sea vessels. On the collier or short-voyage vessel the crew was necessarily a small one, and the shanty was more or less of a makeshift, adapted to the capacity of the limited numbers of the crew. Purely commercial reasons precluded the engagement of any shantyman specially distinguished for his musical attainments. Consequently, so far as the shanty was concerned, 'any old thing would do.' On the Southspainer, however, things were very different. The shantyman was usually a person of considerable musical importance, who sang his songs in a more or less finished manner; his melodies were clean, clear-cut things, without any of the folk-songer's quavers and wobbles. I heard them in the 'seventies and 'eighties before the sailing-ship had vanished, consequently I give them as they were then sung—undisfigured and unobscured by the mixture of twirls, quavers, and hiccups one hears from octogenarian mariners who attempt them to-day.

METHOD OF SINGING

So far as the music was concerned, a shanty was a song with a chorus. The song was rendered by one singer, called the shantyman, and the chorus by the sailors who performed their work in time with the music. So far as the words were concerned there was usually a stereotyped opening of one or more verses. For all succeeding verses the shantyman improvized words, and his topics were many and varied, the most appreciated naturally being personal allusions to the crew and officers, sarcastic criticism on the quality of the food, wistful references to the good time coming on shore, etc. There was no need for any connection or relevancy between one verse or another, nor were rhymes required. The main thing that mattered was that the rhythm should be preserved and that the words should be such as would keep the workers merry or interested. Once the stereotyped verses were got rid of and the improvization began, things became so intimate and personal as to be unprintable. It was a curious fact that such shanty words as lent themselves most to impropriety were wedded to tunes either of fine virility or haunting sweetness.

For 'pull-and-haul' shanties the shantyman took up his position near the workers and announced the shanty, sometimes by singing the first line. This established the tune to which they were to supply the chorus. For capstan shanties he usually did the same. He frequently sat on the capstan, but so far as I can learn he more usually took up his position on or against the knightheads. The importance of the shantyman could not be overestimated. A good shantyman with a pretty wit was worth his weight in gold. He was a privileged person, and was excused all work save light or odd jobs.

THE WORDS OF SHANTIES

I have already noted the shanties which were derived from popular songs, also the type which contained a definite narrative. Except where a popular song was adapted, the form was usually rhymed or more often unrhymed couplets. The topics were many and varied, but the chief ones were: (1) popular heroes such as Napoleon, and 'Santy Anna.' That the British sailor of the eighteenth century should hate every Frenchman and yet make a hero of Bonaparte is one of the mysteries which has never been explained. Another mystery is the fascination which Antonio Lopez de Santa Anna (1795-1876) exercised over the sailor. He was one of the many Mexican 'Presidents' and was defeated [Pg xi] by the American General Taylor in 1847. That did not prevent the British sailor presenting him in the light of an invariable victor until he was led out to be shot (he really died a natural death) by persons unknown. (2) The sailor had mythical heroes too, e.g. 'Ranzo,' already mentioned, and 'Stormy,' who was the theme of many shanties. No sailor could ever give the least explanation of them, and so they remain the last echoes of long forgotten sagas. (3) High-sounding, poetic, or mysterious words, such as 'Lowlands,' 'Shenandoah,' 'Rolling river,' 'Hilo,' 'Mobile Bay,' 'Rio Grande,' had a great fascination, as their constant recurrence in many shanties shows. (4) The sailor also sang much of famous ships, such as 'The Flying Cloud,' 'The Henry Clay,' or 'The Victory,' and famous lines, such as 'The Black Ball.' Even famous shipowners were celebrated in song, as witness 'Mr. John Tapscott,' in 'We're all bound to go.' (5) Love affairs, in which 'Lizer Lee' and other damsels constantly figured, were an endless topic. (6) But chiefly did Jack sing of affairs connected with his ship. He never sang of 'the rolling main,' 'the foaming billows,' 'the storm clouds,' etc. These are the stock-in-trade of the landsman; they were too real for the sailor to sing about. He had the instinct of the primitive man which forbids mention of natural forces of evil omen. But intimate or humorous matters such as the failings of his officers, the quality of the food, the rate of pay, or other grievances were treated with vigour and emphasis. Like the Britisher of to-day, he would put up with any hardship so long as he were permitted to grouse about it. The shantyman gave humorous expression to this grousing, which deprived it of the element of sulks. Steam let off in this way was a wholesome preventive of mutiny.

The choruses were usually jingles, with no relevance save maintenance of the rhythm.

One feature of the words may be noted. The sailor's instinct for romance was so strong that in his choruses, at least, no matter how 'hair-curling' the solo might be, he always took the crude edge off the concrete and presented it as an abstraction if possible. For example, he knew perfectly well that one meaning of 'to blow' was to knock or kick. He knew that discipline in Yankee packets was maintained by corporeal methods, so much so that the Mates, to whom the function of knocking the 'packet rats' about was delegated, were termed first, second, and third 'blowers,' or strikers, and in the shanty he sang 'Blow the man down.' 'Knock' or 'kick,' as I have recently seen in a printed collection, was too crudely realistic for him. In like manner the humorous title, 'Hog's-eye,' veiled the coarse intimacy of the term which it represented. And that is where, when collecting shanties from the 'longshore' mariner of to-day, I find him, if he is uneducated, so tiresome. He not only wants to explain to me as a landsman the exact meaning (which I know already) of terms which the old type of sailor, with his natural delicacy, avoided discussing, but he tries where possible to work them into his shanty, a thing the sailor of old time never did. So that when one sees in print expressions which sailors did not use, it is presumptive evidence that the collector has been imposed upon by a salt of the 'sea lawyer' type.

Perhaps I ought to make this point clearer. Folk-song collecting was once an artistic pursuit. Now it has become a flourishing industry of high commercial value. From the commercial point of view it is essential that results should be printed and circulated as widely as possible. Some knowledge of seamanship is an absolute necessity where folk-shanties are concerned. The mere collector nowadays does not possess that knowledge; it is confined to those who have had practical experience of the sea, but who will never print their experiences. The mere collector *must* print his versions. What is unprinted must remain unknown; what is printed is therefore accepted as authoritative, however misleading it may be. Many highly educated men, of whom Captain Whall is the type, have followed the sea. It is from them that the only really trustworthy information is forthcoming. But so far as I can judge, it is uneducated men who appear to sing to collectors nowadays, and I have seen many a quiet smile on the lips of the educated sailor when he is confronted with printed versions of the uneducated seaman's performances. For example, one of the best known of all shanties is 'The Hog's-eye man'; I have seen this entitled 'The Hog-eyed man,' and even 'The Ox-eyed man.' Every old sailor knew the meaning of the term. Whall and Bullen, who were both sailors, use the correct expression, 'Hog-eye.' The majority of sailors of my acquaintance called it 'Hog's-eye.' Did decency permit I could show conclusively how Whall and Bullen are right and the mere collector wrong. It must suffice, however, for me to say that the term 'Hog's-eye' or 'Hog-eye' had nothing whatever to do with the optic of the 'man' who was sung about. I could multiply instances, but this one is typical and must suffice.

We hear a great deal of the coarseness and [Pg xii] even lewdness of the shanty, but I could wish a little more stress were laid on the sailor's natural delicacy. Jack was always a gentleman in feeling. Granted his drinking, cursing, and amours—but were not these, until Victorian times, the hall-mark of every gentleman ashore? The Rabelaisian jokes of the shantyman were solos, the sound of which would not travel far beyond the little knot of workers who chuckled over them. The choruses—shouted out by the whole working party—would be heard all over the ship and even penetrate ashore if she were in port. Hence, in not a single instance do the choruses of any shanty contain a coarse expression.

EDITORIAL METHODS

As regards the tunes, I have adhered to the principle of giving each one as it was sung by some individual singer. This method has not been applied to the words. Consequently the verses of any given shanty may have derived from any number of singers. Since there was no connection or relevancy between the different verses of a shanty, the only principle I have adhered to is that whatever verses are set down should have been sung to me at some time or other by some sailor or other.

Of course I have had to camouflage many unprintable expressions, and old sailors will readily recognize where this has been done. Sometimes a whole verse (after the first line) has needed camouflage, and the method adopted is best expressed as follows:

  There was a young lady of Gloucester
Who couldn't eat salt with her egg,
And when she sat down
She could never get up,
And so the poor dog had none.

As regards the accompaniments, I have been solely guided by the necessity of preserving the character of the melodies in all their vigour and vitality, and have tried, even in obviously modal tunes, not to obscure their breeziness by academic treatment.

ACKNOWLEDGMENTS

Amongst those to whom I owe thanks, I must number the Editors of *The Music Student* and *Music and Letters*, for allowing me to incorporate in this Preface portions of articles which I have written for them. Also to Capt. W. J. Dowdy, both for singing shanties to me himself, and affording me facilities for interviewing inmates of the Royal Albert Institution, over which he presides. I also wish to express my gratitude to those sailors who have in recent years sung shanties to me, especially Capt. R.W. Robertson, Mr. Geo. Vickers, Mr. Richard Allen, of Seahouses, and Mr. F.B. Mayoss. And last, but not least, to Mr. Morley Roberts, who has not only sung shanties to me, but has also given me the benefit of his ripe nautical experience.

R.R.T.
Hampstead, 1921.
[Pg xiii]

NOTES ON THE SHANTIES

1. BILLY BOY

This is undoubtedly a coast song 'made into a shanty.' I heard it in Northumberland, both on shore and in ships, when I was a boy. The theme of a 'Boy Billy' seems common to folk-songs in different parts of the country. The tunes are different, and the words vary, but the topic is always the same: 'Billy' is asked where he has been all the day; he replies that he has been courting; he is then questioned as to the qualifications of his *inamorata* as a housewife. Dr. Vaughan-Williams's 'My Boy Billie' is in print and well known, as is also Mr. Cecil Sharp's 'My Boy Willie' ['English Folk-Songs,' vol. i, page 98]. I have also collected different versions in Warwickshire and Somerset. The version of line 1, page 3, bars 2 and 3, is older than the one given in my arrangement for male-voice chorus (Curwen Edition 50572), so, upon consideration, I decided to give it here. There are many more verses, but they are not printable, nor do they readily lend themselves to camouflage. The tune has not appeared in print until now.

2. BOUND FOR THE RIO GRANDE

The variants of this noble tune are legion. But this version, which a sailor uncle taught me, has been selected, as I think it the most beautiful of all. I used to notice, even as a boy, how it seemed to inspire the shantyman to sentimental flights of *Heimweh* that at times came perilously near poetry. The words of the well-known song, 'Where are you going to, my pretty maid?' were frequently sung to this shanty, and several sailors have told me that they had also used the words of the song known as 'The Fishes.' Capt. Whall gives 'The Fishes' on pages 96 and 97 of his book, and says that the words were, in his time, sometimes used to the tune of 'Blow the man down.'

3. GOOD-BYE, FARE YE WELL

This is one of the best beloved of shanties. So strongly did its sentiment appeal to sailors that one never heard the shantyman extemporize a coarse verse to it. Whall prints a version, page 71.

4. JOHNNY COME DOWN TO HILO

This is clearly of negro origin. I learnt several variants of it, but for its present form I am indebted to Capt. W. J. Dowdy.

5. CLEAR THE TRACK, LET THE BULLGINE RUN

The tune was a favourite in Yankee Packets. It does not appear in Whall. 'Bullgine' was American negro slang for 'engine.' I picked up this version in boyhood from Blyth seamen.

6. LOWLANDS

For another version see Whall (page 80), who says it is of American origin and comes from the cotton ports of the old Southern States. It was well known to every sailor down to the time of the China Clippers. My version is that of Capt. John Runciman, who belonged to that period. I have seldom found it known to sailors who took to the sea after the early seventies. The tune was sung in very free time and with great solemnity. It is almost impossible to reproduce in print the elusive subtlety of this haunting melody. In North-country ships the shantyman used to make much of the theme of a dead lover appearing in the night. There were seldom any rhymes, and the air was indescribably touching when humoured by a good hand. A 'hoosier,' by the way, is a cotton stevedore. An interesting point about this shanty is that, whether by accident or design, it exhibits a rhythmic device commonly practised by mediæval composers, known as *proportio sesquialtera*. Expressed in modern notation it would mean the interpolation of bars of three-four time in the course of a composition which was in six-eight time. The number of quavers would, of course, be the same in each bar; but the rhythm would be different. The barring here adopted does not show this.

7. SALLY BROWN

For another version of this universally known shanty see Whall, page 64. Although its musical form is that of a halliard shanty, it was always used for the capstan. I never heard it used for any other purpose than heaving the anchor. The large-sized notes given in the last bar are those which most sailors sing to me nowadays; the small ones are those which I most frequently heard when a boy.

8. SANTY ANNA

This fine shanty was a great favourite, and in defiance of all history the sailor presents 'Santy Anna' in the light of an invariable victor. The truth is that Antonio Lopez de Santa Anna [Pg xiv] (1795-1876) was the last President of Mexico before the annexation by America of California, Texas, and New Mexico. He defeated the Spaniards at Zampico, and held Vera Cruz against the French, but was badly beaten at Molina del Rey by the United States Army under General Taylor (1847). He was recalled to the Presidency in 1853, but overthrown in 1855. He attempted to overturn the Republic in 1867; was captured and sentenced to death, but was pardoned on condition that he left the country. He retired to the United States until 1872, when a general amnesty allowed his return to Mexico. Like other Mexican Presidents, he lived a stormy life, but unlike most of them he died a natural death. Whall gives a version on page 89.

9. SHENANDOAH

This is one of the most famous of all shanties. I never met a sailor to whom it was unknown, nor have I ever found any two who sang it exactly alike. This version (sung to me by Capt. Robertson) is almost, but not quite, identical with the one I learnt as a boy. Shenandoah (English seamen usually pronounced it 'Shannandore') was a celebrated Indian chief after whom an American town is named. A branch of the Potomac river bears the same name. The tune was always sung with great feeling and in very free rhythm. Whall gives a version on page 1.

10. STORMALONG JOHN

This is one of the many shanties with 'Stormy' as their hero. Whatever other verses were extemporized, those relating to digging his grave with a silver spade, and lowering him down with a golden chain, were rarely omitted. Other favourite verses were:

(*a*) I wish I was old Stormy's son.
(*b*) I'd build a ship a thousand ton.

Who 'Stormy' was is undiscoverable, but more than a dozen shanties mourn him.

11. THE HOG'S-EYE MAN

Of the numberless versions of this shanty I have chosen that of Capt. Robertson as being the most representative. Of the infinite number of verses to this fine tune hardly one is printable. There has been much speculation as to the origin of the title. As a boy my curiosity was piqued by reticence, evasion, or declarations of ignorance, whenever I asked the meaning of the term. It was only in later life that I learnt it from Mr. Morley Roberts. His explanation made it clear why every *sailor* called it either 'hog-eye' or 'hog's-eye,' and why only *landsmen* editors ever get the word wrong. One collector labels the shanty 'The hog-eyed man,' and another goes still further wide of the mark by calling it 'The ox-eyed man.' The remarks on this shanty in the Preface will show the absurdity of both titles. That is all the explanation I am at liberty to give in print. Whall gives the shanty on page 118, his version differing but slightly from Capt. Robertson's.

12. THE WILD GOOSE SHANTY

This I learnt from Capt. John Runciman. Allusions to 'The Wild Goose Nation' occur in many shanties, but I never obtained any clue to the meaning (if any) of the term. The verse about 'huckleberry hunting' was rarely omitted, but I never heard that particular theme further developed. Whall gives another version (in six-eight time) on page 131.

13. WE'RE ALL BOUND TO GO

I used to hear this tune constantly on the Tyne. It is one of the few shanties which preserved a definite narrative, but each port seems to have offered variants on the names of the ships that were 'bound for Amerikee.' 'Mr. Tapscott' was the head of a famous line of emigrant ships. The last word in verse 5 was always pronounced *male*. This has led to many shantymen treating it not as *meal*, but as the *mail* which the ship carried. As the shanty is full of Irish allusions, the probabilities are that the word was *meal*, to which the sailor gave what he considered to be the Irish pronunciation. Whenever I heard the shanty it was given with an attempt at Irish pronunciation throughout. Capt. Whall (page 79) gives additional colour to the supposition that this was a general practice, for his version of verse 6 runs:

'Bad luck unto them *say*-boys,
Bad luck to them I say;
They broke into me *say*-chest
And they stole me clothes away.'

14. WHAT SHALL WE DO WITH THE DRUNKEN SAILOR?

This fine tune—in the first Mode—was always a great favourite. Although mostly used for windlass or capstan, Sir Walter Runciman tells me that he frequently sang to it for 'hand-over-hand' hauling. Whall gives it on page 107 under the title 'Early in the morning.' It is one of the few shanties that were sung in quick time.

15. BLOW, MY BULLY BOYS

This shanty has been included in every collection that I know of. (See Whall, page 91.) [Pg xv] Most of my sailor relatives sang the last line thus:

Her masts and yards they shine like sil - ver.

16. BLOW THE MAN DOWN

This is the shanty which is perhaps the best known among landsmen. 'Winchester Street' is in South Shields, and in the old days was the aristocratic quarter where only persons of high distinction—such as shipowners, and 'Southspainer' skippers—lived. Whall gives the shanty on page 92.

17. CHEER'LY, MEN

This is a very well-known shanty, and the variants of it are endless. This particular version was sung to me by Capt. R.W. Robertson. It differs but slightly from the version which I originally learnt from Sir Walter Runciman. Very few of the words were printable, and old sailors who read my version will no doubt chuckle over the somewhat pointless continuation of the verses concerning Kitty Carson and Polly Riddle. They will, of course, see the point of my having supplied a Chopinesque accompaniment to such a shanty.

18. GOOD MORNING, LADIES ALL

The title belongs to other shanties as well; but, so far as I know, this tune has never been printed until now. I learnt it from Northumbrian sailors when a very small boy, and have never heard of its use in any other than Blyth and Tyne ships. It may be a Northumbrian air, but from such knowledge as I have gleaned of Northumbrian folk-tunes, I incline to the conjecture that it may have been picked up in more southern latitudes by some Northumbrian seaman.

19. HANGING JOHNNY

This cheery riot of gore is wedded to the most plaintive of tunes, and is immortalized by Masefield in his 'Sailor's Garland.' Nowadays one occasionally meets unhumorous longshore sailormen who endeavour to temper its fury to the shorn landsman by palming off a final verse, which gives one to understand that the previous stanzas have been only 'Johnny's' little fun, and which makes him bleat:

'They said I hanged for money,
But I never hanged nobody.'

I also possess a shanty collection where the words have so clearly shocked the editor that he has composed an entirely fresh set. These exhibit 'Johnny' as a spotless moralist, who would never *really* hang his parents, but would only operate (in a Pickwickian sense of course) on naughty and unworthy people:

'I'd hang a noted liar,
I'd hang a bloated friar.'
'I'd hang a brutal mother,
I'd hang her and no other.'
'I'd hang to make things jolly,
I'd hang all wrong and folly.'

Imagine a shantyman (*farceur* as he ever was) making for edification in that style!

20. HILO SOMEBODY

This is another of the shanties I learnt as a boy from Blyth sailors, and which has never been printed before. I fancy that 'blackbird' and 'crew' must be a perversion of 'blackbird and *crow*,' as the latter figure of speech occurs in other shanties.

21. OH, RUN, LET THE BULLGINE RUN

The reference to the 'Bullgine' seems to suggest Transatlantic origin. There were endless verses, but no attempt at narrative beyond a recital of the names of places from which and to which they were 'running.' This version was sung to me by Mr. F.B. Mayoss, a seaman who sailed in the old China Clippers.

22. REUBEN RANZO

Alden gives this version, and I fancy it may have once been fairly general, as several of my relatives used to sing it. The version I mostly heard from other sailors, however, began:

[Pg xvi]
Who Ranzo was must ever remain a mystery. Capt. Whall suggests that the word might be a corruption of Lorenzo, since Yankee Whalers took many Portuguese men from the Azores, where Lorenzo would have been a common enough name. He adds that in his time the shanty was always sung to the regulation words, and that 'when the story was finished there was no attempt at improvization; the text was, I suppose, considered sacred.' He further says that he never heard any variation from the words which he gives.

I think he is right about the absence of improvization on extraneous topics, but I used to hear a good deal of improvization on the subject of Ranzo himself. I knew at least three endings of the story: (1) where the captain took him into the cabin, 'larned him navigation,' and eventually married him to his daughter; (2) where Ranzo's hatred of ablutions caused the indignant crew to throw him overboard; (3) where the story ended with the lashes received, not for his dirty habits, but for a theft:

'We gave him lashes thirty
For stealin' the captain's turkey.'

I have also heard many extemporaneous verses relating his adventures among the denizens of the deep after he was thrown overboard.

23. THE DEAD HORSE

This shanty was used both for hauling and for pumping ship. It seems to have had its origin in a rite which took place after the crew had 'worked off the dead horse.' The circumstances were these: Before any voyage, the crew received a month's pay in advance, which, needless to say, was spent ashore before the vessel sailed. Jack's first month on sea was therefore spent in clearing off his advance, which he called working off the dead horse. The end of that payless period was celebrated with a solemn ceremony: a mass of straw, or whatever other combustibles were to hand, was made up into a big bundle, which sometimes did, and more often did not, resemble a horse. This was dragged round the deck by all hands, the shanty being sung meanwhile. The perambulation completed, the dead horse was lighted and hauled up, usually to the main-yardarm, and when the flames had got a good hold, the rope was cut and the blazing mass fell into the sea, amid shouts of jubilation.

24. TOM'S GONE TO HILO

This beautiful tune was very popular. I have chosen the version sung to me by Mr. George Vickers, although in the first chorus it differs somewhat from the version I learnt as a boy:

25. WHISKY JOHNNY

This Bacchanalian chant was a prime favourite. Every sailor knew it, and every collection includes some version of it.

26. BONEY WAS A WARRIOR

I never met a seaman who has not hoisted topsails to this shanty. Why Jack should have made a hero of Boney (he frequently pronounced it 'Bonny') is a mystery, except perhaps that, as a sailor, he realized the true desolation of imprisonment on a sea-girt island, and his sympathies went out to the lonely exile accordingly. Or it may have been the natural liking of the Briton for any enemy who proved himself a 'bonny fechter.'

27. JOHNNY BOKER

This popular shanty was sometimes used for bunting-up a sail, but more usually for 'sweating-up.' Although I have allowed the last note its full musical value, it was not prolonged in this manner aboard ship. As it coincided with the pull, it usually sounded more like a staccato grunt.

28. HAUL AWAY, JOE

The major version of this shanty (which appears in Part II) was more general in the last days of the sailing ship; but this minor version (certainly the most beautiful of them) is the one which I used to hear on the Tyne. The oldest of my sailor relatives never sang any other. This inclines me to the belief that it is the earlier version. The verses extemporized to this shanty were endless, but those concerning the Nigger Girl and King Louis never seem to have been omitted. As in No. 27, I have allowed the last [Pg xvii] note its full musical value, but aboard ship it was sung in the same manner as No. 27.

29. WE'LL HAUL THE BOWLIN'

This was the most popular shanty for 'sweating-up.' There are many variants of it. The present version I learnt from Capt. John Runciman. In this shanty no attempt was ever made to sing the last word. It was always shouted.

30. PADDY DOYLE'S BOOTS

This shanty differs from all others, as (*a*) it was sung *tutti* throughout; (*b*) it had only one verse, which was sung over and over again; and (*c*) it was used for one operation and one operation only, viz. bunting up the foresail or mainsail in furling. In this operation the canvas of the sail was folded intensively until it formed a smooth conical bundle. This was called a bunt, and a strong collective effort (at the word 'boots') was required to get it on to the yard.

Although the same verse was sung over and over again, very occasionally a different text would be substituted, which was treated in the same manner. Capt. Whall gives two alternatives, which were sometimes used:

'We'll all drink brandy and gin,'
and—
'We'll all shave under the chin.'

Mr. Morley Roberts also told me that a variant in his ship was—

'We'll all throw dirt at the cook.'
[Pg 2]

THE SHANTY BOOK.

PART I.

Transcriber's Note: A vowel with an umlaut indicates that the word or syllable has two dots over it in the original text, presumably to indicate that it should be prolonged when sung. See the Glossary below.

1. Billy Boy.

(NORTHUMBRIAN CAPSTAN SHANTY.)

[Listen]

[Pg 3]
Copyright, 1921, by J. Curwen & Sons Ltd.

1. Where hev ye been äal the day,
Billy Boy, Billy Boy?
Where hev ye been äal the day, me Billy Boy?
I've been walkin' äal the day
With me charmin' Nancy Grey,
And me Nancy kittl'd me fancy
Oh me charmin' Billy Boy.

2. Is she fit to be yor wife
Billy Boy, Billy Boy?
Is she fit to be yor wife, me Billy Boy?
She's as fit to be me wife
As the fork is to the knife
And me Nancy, *etc.*

3. Can she cook a bit o' steak
Billy Boy, Billy Boy?
Can she cook a bit o' steak, me Billy Boy?
She can cook a bit o' steak,
Aye, and myek a gairdle cake
And me Nancy, *etc.*

4. Can she myek an Irish Stew
Billy Boy, Billy Boy?
Can she myek an Irish Stew, me Billy Boy?
She can myek an Irish Stew
Aye, and "Singin' Hinnies" too.
And me Nancy, *etc.*

Glossary:—

äal = all. Pronounced to rhyme with "shall" only the vowel must be very much prolonged.

kittled = tickled.

myek = make.

gairdle cake = girdle cake, i.e. a cake baked on a griddle.

Singin' Hinnies—i.e. a species of Sally Lunn teacake only larger. Usually plentifully besprinkled with currants, in which case it is designated by pitmen as "Singin' Hinnies wi' smäa co fizzors" (small coal fizzers.)

[Pg 4]

2. Bound for the Rio Grande.

(WINDLASS AND CAPSTAN SHANTY.)

[Listen]

[Pg 5]

1. I'll sing you a song of the fish of the sea.
Oh Rio.
I'll sing you a song of the fish of the sea
And we're bound for the Rio Grande.
Then away love, away,
'Way down Rio,
So fare ye well my pretty young gel.
For we're bound for the Rio Grande.

2. Sing good-bye to Sally, and good-bye to Sue, Oh Rio, *etc.*
And you who are listening, good-bye to you. And we're bound, *etc.*

3. Our ship

went

sailing out over the Bar

And

we

pointed her nose for the South-er-en Star.

4. Farewell and adieu to you ladies of Spain

And

we're

all of us coming to see you again.

5. I

said

fare

well

to

Kitty my dear,

And

she

waved her white hand as we passed the South Pier.

6. The oak, and the ash, and the bonny birk tree
They're all growing green in the North Countrie.

[Pg 6]

3. Good-bye, fare ye well.

[Listen]

[Pg 7]

1. I thought I heard the old man say

Good-bye, fare ye well,
Good-bye, fare ye well.
I thought I heard the old man say,
Hooray my boys we're homeward bound.

   2. We're homeward bound, I hear the sound. (*twice*)

   3. We sailed away to Mobile Bay. (*twice*)

   4. But now we're bound for Portsmouth Town. (*twice*)

   5. And soon we'll be ashore again. (*twice*)

   6. I kissed my Kitty upon the pier
And

𝅘𝅥𝅮

it's

𝅘𝅥𝅮

oh to see you again my dear.

   7. We're homeward bound, and I hear the sound. (*twice*)

[Pg 8]

4. Johnny come down to Hilo.

(WINDLASS AND CAPSTAN.)

[Listen]
[Pg 9]

1. I nebber see de like since I bin born,
When a big buck nigger wid de sea boots on,
Says "Johnny come down to Hilo.
Poor old man."
Oh wake her, oh, shake her,
Oh wake dat gel wid de blue dress on,
When Johnny comes down to Hilo.
Poor old man.

   2. I lub a little gel across de sea,
She's a Badian [1] beauty and she sez to me,
"Oh Johnny," *etc.*

   3. Oh was you ebber down in Mobile Bay
Where dey screws de cotton on a summer day?
When Johnny, *etc.*

   4. Did

𝅘𝅥𝅮

you

𝅘𝅥𝅮

ebber see de ole Plantation Boss
And de long-tailed filly and de big black hoss?
When Johnny, *etc.*

   5. I nebber seen de like since I bin born
When a big buck nigger wid de sea boots on,
Says "Johnny come down," *etc.*

[Pg 10]

5. Clear the track, let the Bullgine run.

(WINDLASS AND CAPSTAN.)

[Listen]
[Pg 11]

1. Oh, the smartest clipper you can find.
Ah ho Way-oh, are you most done.
Is the Marget Evans of the Blue Cross Line.
So clear the track, let the Bullgine run.
Tibby Hey rig a jig in a jaunting car.
Ah ho Way-oh, are you most done.
With Lizer Lee all on my knee.
So clear the track, let the Bullgine run.

   2. Oh the Marget Ev

𝅘𝅥𝅮

ans

𝅘𝅥𝅮

of

𝅘𝅥𝅮

the

𝅘𝅥𝅮

Blue Cross Line
She's nev

𝅘𝅥𝅮

er

𝅘𝅥𝅮

a day behind her time.

3. Oh the gels are walking on the pier
And

I'll

soon be home to you, my dear.
4. Oh when I come home across the sea,
It's Lizer you will marry me.
5. Öh shake her, wake her,

be

fore

we're

gone;

Oh fetch that gel with the blue dress on.
6. Oh I thought I heard the skipper say
"We'll keep the brig three points away."
7. Oh the smartest clipper you can find
Is the Marget Ev

ans

of

the

Blue Cross Line.
[Pg 12]

6. Lowlands away.

(WINDLASS AND CAPSTAN.)

[Listen]
[Pg 13]
[Pg 14]
[Pg 15]

(INTRODUCTION.)
Lowlands, Lowlands,
Away my John,
Lowlands, away,
I heard them say,
My dollar and a half a day.
1. A dollar and a half a day is a Hoosier's pay.

Lowlands, Lowlands,
Away my John.
A dollar and a half a day is very good pay.
My dollar and a half a day.
2. Oh was you ever in Mobile Bay.

Lowlands, Lowlands,
Away my John.
Screwing the cotton by the day.
My dollar and a half a day.
3. All in the night my true love came,
Lowlands, Lowlands,
Away my John.
All in the night my true love came.
My dollar and a half a day.
4. She came to me all in my sleep.
(*twice*)
5. And hër eyes were white my love.
(*twice*)
6. And then I knew my love was dead.
(*twice*)
[Pg 16]

7. Sally Brown

(WINDLASS AND CAPSTAN.)

[Listen]

[Pg 17]

1. Sally Brown she's a bright Mulatter.
Way Ay-y Roll and go.
She drinks rum and chews terbacker.

Spend my money on Sally Brown.
  2. Sally Brown shë has a daughter
Sent me sailin' 'cross the water.
3. Seven long years Ï courted Sally. (*twice*)
4. Sally Brown I'm bound to leave you
Sally Brown I'll not deceive you.
5. Sally she's a 'Badian' beauty. (*twice*)
6. Sally lives on the old plantation
She belongs the Wild Goose Nation.
7. Sally Brown is a bright Mulatter
She drinks rum and chews terbacker.
  [Pg 18]

8. Santy Anna.

(WINDLASS AND CAPSTAN.)

[Listen]

[Pg 19]

  1. Oh Santy Anna won the day.
Way-Ah, me Santy Anna.
Oh Santy Anna won the day.
All on the plains of Mexico.
  2. He beat the Prooshans fairly. Way-Ah, *etc.*
And whacked the British nearly. All on, *etc.*
3. He was a rorty gineral;
A rorty snorty gineral.

4. They took him out and shöt him.
Oh when shall we forgët him.
5. Oh Santy Anna won the day
And Gin'ral Taylor run away.
  [Pg 20]

9. Shenandoah. [2]

(WINDLASS AND CAPSTAN.)
[Listen]

[Pg 21]

  1. Oh Shenandoah, I long to hear you.
Away you rolling river.
Oh Shenandoah, I long to hear you.

Away, I'm bound to go
'Cross the wide Missouri.
  2. Oh Shenandoah, I love your daughter. (*twice*)
3. 'Tis seven long years since last I see thee. (*twice*)
4. Oh Shenandoah, I took a notion
To sail across the stormy ocean.
5. Oh Shenandoah, I'm bound to leave you.
Oh Shenandoah, I'll not deceive you.
6. Oh Shenandoah, I long to hear you. (*twice*)
  [Pg 22]

10. Stormalong John.

(WINDLASS AND CAPSTAN.)
[Listen]

[Pg 23]

  1. Oh poor old Stormy's dead and gone.
Storm along boys,
Storm along.
Oh poor old Stormy's dead and gone.

Ah-ha, come along, get along,
Stormy along John.
   2. I dug his grave with a silver spade. (*twice*)
   3. I lower'd him down with a golden chain. (*twice*)
   4. I carried him away to Mobile Bay. (*twice*)
   5. Oh poor old Stormy's dead and gone. (*twice*)
[Pg 24]

11. The Hog's-eye Man.

(WINDLASS AND CAPSTAN.)
[Listen]

[Pg 25]

   1. Oh the hog's-eye man is the man for me,
He were raised way down in Tennessee.
Oh hog's eye, oh.
Row the boat ashore for the hog's-eye.
Steady on a jig with a hog's-eye oh,
She wants the hog's-eye man.
   2. Oh who's been here while I've been gone?

Söme big buck nigger,
with his sea boots on? [3]
3. Oh bring me down mÿ riding cane,
For I'm off to see my darling Jane.
   4. Oh Jenny's in the garden a-picking peas,
   And her golden hair's hanging down to her knees.
   5. Oh a hog's-eye ship, and a hog's-eye crew,
And a hog's-eye mate, and a skipper too.
[Pg 26]

12. The Wild Goose Shanty.

(WINDLASS AND CAPSTAN.)
[Listen]
[Pg 27]

   1. I'm the Shanty-man of the Wild Goose Nation.
Tibby Way-ay Hioha!
I've left my wife on a big plantation.
Hilo my Ranzo Hay!
   2. Now a long farewell to the old plantation. (*twice*)
3. And a long farewell to the Wild Goose Nation. (*twice*)
   4. Oh the boys and the girls went a huckleberry hunting. (*twice*)
   5. Then good-bye and farewell

yöu rolling river. (*twice*)
6. I'm the Shanty-man of the Wild Goose Nation.
I've left my wife on a big plantation.
[Pg 28]

13. We're all bound to go.

(WINDLASS AND CAPSTAN.)
[Listen]

[Pg 29]

1. Oh Johnny was a rover
And to-day he sails away.
Heave away, my Johnny,
Heave away-ay.
Oh Johnny was a rover
And to-day he sails away.
Heave away my bully boys,
We're all bound to go.
  2. As I was walking out one day,
Down by the Albert Dock.
Heave away, &c.
I heard an emigrant Irish girl
Conversing with Tapscott.
Heave away, &c.
3. "Good mornin', Mister Tapscott, sir,"

"Good morn, my gel," sez he,
"It's have you got a Packet Ship
All bound for Amerikee?"
4. "Oh yes, I've got a Packet Ship,
I *have* got one or two.
I've got the *Jenny Walker*
And I've got the *Kangeroo*."
5. "I've got the *Jenny Walker*
And to-day she does set sail,
With five and fifty emigrants
  And a thousand bags o' male." [4]
  6. Bad luck to thim Irish sailor boys,
Bad luck to thim I say.
  For they all got drunk, and broke into me bunk
And stole me clo'es away.
  [Pg 30]

14. What shall we do with the drunken sailor?

(WINDLASS AND CAPSTAN.)
[Listen]
[Pg 31]

1. What shall we do with the drunken sailor,
What shall we do with the drunken sailor,
What shall we do with the drunken sailor
Early in the morning?
Hooray and up she rises,
Hooray and up she rises,
Hooray and up she rises
Early in the morning.
  2. Put him in the long-boat until he's sober. (*thrice*)
  3. Pull out the plug änd wet him all over. (*thrice*)
  4. Put him in the scuppers with a hose-pipe on him. (*thrice*)
  5. Heave

him

by the leg in a running bowlin'. (*thrice*)
  6. Tie

him

to the taff

rail

when she's yard-arm under. (*thrice*)
  [Pg 32]

15. Blow my bully boys.

(HALLIARD SHANTY.)
[Listen]

  1. A Yankee ship came down the river,
Blow, boys blow.
Her masts and yards they shine like silver.
Blow my bully boys blow.
  2. And how d'ye know she'

s a

Yankee packet?
The Stars and Stripes they fly above her.
3. And who d'ye think was skipper of her. (*twice*)
4. 'Twas Dandy Jim, the one-eyed nigger;
  'Twas Dandy Jim, with

his

bully figure.
5. And what d'ye think they had for dinner?
Why bullock's lights and donkey's liver.
6. And what d'ye think they had for supper?
Why weevilled bread and Yankee leather.
7. Then blow my boys, and blow together.
And blow my boys for better weather.
8. A Yankee ship came down the river.
Her masts and yards they shine like silver.
  [Pg 34]

16. Blow the man down.

(HALLIARDS.)
[Listen]

  [Pg 35]

  1. Oh blow the man down, bullies, blow the man down.
To me Way-ay, blow the man down.
Oh blow the man down, bullies, blow him away.
Oh gimme some time to blow the man

down.
  2. We went over the Bar on the thirteenth of May.
To me Way-ay, blow the man down.
The Galloper jumped, and the gale came away.
Oh gimme some time to blow the man down.
  3. Oh the rags they was gone, and the chains they was jammed,
    And

the

skipper sez he, "Let the weather be hanged."
4. Äs I was a-walking down Winchester Street,
A saucy young damsel I happened to meet.
5. Ï sez to her, "Polly, and how d'you do?"
Sez she, "None the better for seein' of you."
6. Oh, it's sailors is tinkers, and tailors is men.
    And

we're

all of us coming to see you again.
7. So we'll blow the man up, and we'll blow the man down.
    And

we'll

blow him away into Liverpool Town.
  [Pg 36]

17. Cheer'ly men. [5]

(HALLIARDS.)

[Listen]

[Pg 37]

1. Oh, Nancy Dawson, I-Oh.
Chee-lee men.
She robb'd the Bo'sun, I-Oh.
Chee-lee men.
That was a caution, I-Oh.
Chee-lee men.
Oh Hauly, I-Oh,
Chee-lee men.
  2. Oh Sally Racket. I-Oh, &c.
Pawned my best jacket. I-Oh, &c.
Sold the pawn ticket. I-Oh, &c.
3. Oh Kitty Carson
Jilted the parson,
Married a mason.
4. Oh Betsy Baker
Lived in Long Acre,
Married a quaker.
5. Oh Jenny Walker
Married a hawker
That was a corker.
6. Oh Polly Riddle
Broke her new fiddle.
Right through the middle.

18. Good morning, ladies all.

(HALLIARDS.)

[Listen]

[Pg 38]

[Pg 39]

1. Now a long good-bye to you, my dear,
With a heave-oh haul.
And a last farewell, and a long farewell.
And good morning, ladies all.
  2. For we're outward bound to New York town;
With a heave, *etc.*
And you'll wave to us till the sun goes down.
And good morning, *etc.*
3. Änd when we get to New York town,
Oh it's there we'll drink, and sorrows drown.
4. When we're back once möre in London Docks,
All the pretty girls will come in flocks.
5. Änd Poll, and Bet, and Sue will say:
"Oh it's here comes Jack with his three years' pay."
6. So a long good-bye to you, my dear,
And a last farewell, and a long farewell.

19. Hanging Johnny.

(HALLIARDS.)

[Listen]

[Pg 40]

[Pg 41]

1. Oh they call me hanging Johnny.
Away, boys, away.
They says I hangs for money.
Oh hang, boys, hang.
  2. Änd first I hanged my daddy. (*twice*)
3. Änd then I hanged my mother,
My sister and my brother.
4. Änd then I hanged my granny. (*twice*)
5. Änd then I hanged my Annie;
I hanged her up see canny. [6]
6. Wë'll hang and haul together;
We'll haul for better weather.
[Pg 42]

20. Hilo somebody.

(HALLIARDS AND INTERCHANGEABLE.)

[Listen]
[Pg 43]

1. The blackbird sang unto our crew.
Hilo boys, Hilo.
The blackbird sang unto our crew.
Oh Hilo somebody, Hilo.
   2. The blackbird sang so sweet to me. (*twice*)
3. We sailed away to Mobile Bay. (*twice*)
4. And now we're bound for London Town. (*twice*)
5. The up aloft this yard must go. (*twice*)
6. I thought I heard the old man say:— "Just one more pull, and then belay."
7. Hooray my boys, we're homeward bound. (*twice*)
8. The blackbird sang unto our crew. (*twice*)
   [Pg 44]

21. Oh run, let the Bullgine run.

(HALLIARDS.)

[Listen]
[Pg 45]

1. Oh we'll run all night till the morning.
Oh run, let the Bullgine run.
Way-yah, Oh-I-Oh, run, let the Bullgine run.
   2. Oh we sailed all day tö Mobile Bay.
3. Oh we sailed all nïght äcross the Bight. [7]
4. Oh we'll run from Dover to Cällis.
5. Öh drive her captäin, drïve her.
6. Öh captain make her nöse blood.
7. She's a dandy packet and a flier too.
8. With a dandy skipper, and a dandy crew.
9. Oh we'll run all nïght till the mörning.
   [Pg 46]

22. Reuben Ranzo.

(HALLIARDS.)

[Listen]
[Pg 47]

1. Oh poor old Reuben Ranzo,
Oh Ranzo boys, Ranzo.
Ah pity poor Reuben Ranzo.
Ranzo boys, Ranzo.
   2. Oh Ranzo was no sailor
He shipped on board a whaler.
3. Old Ranzo couldn't steer her,
Did you
ev
er
hear an
yt
hing queerer?
   4. Oh Ranzo was no beauty
   Why could
n't
he do his duty?
   5. Oh Ranzo washed onc
e a
fortnight
He said it was his birthright.
   6. They triced up
this
man so dirty

And gave him five and thirty. [8]
7. Oh poor old Reuben Ranzo
 Ah pi

ty

poor Reuben Ranzo.
 [Pg 48]

23. The dead horse.

(HALLIARDS, or PUMPING SHIP.)

[Listen]

[Pg 49]

1. A poor old man came riding by.
And they say so, and they hope so.
A poor old man came riding by.
Oh poor old man.
 2. I said "Old man your hoss will die." (*twice*)
3. And if he dies I'll tan his skin. (*twice*)
4. And if he lives you'll ride again. (*twice*)
5. I thought I heard the skipper say. (*twice*)
6. Oh one more pull and then belay. (*twice*)
7. A poor old man came riding by. (*twice*)

[Pg 50]

24. Tom's gone to Hilo.

(HALLIARDS.)

[Listen]

[Pg 51]

1. Tommy's gone and I'll go too,
Away down Hilo.
Oh, Tommy's gone and I'll go too.
Tom's gone to Hilo.
 2. Tommy's gone to Liverpool, Away, &c.
Oh, Tommy's gone to Liverpool,
Tom's gone to Hilo.
3. Tommy's gone to Mobile Bay.
Oh, Tommy's gone to Mobile Bay.
4. Tommy's gone, what shall I do?
Oh, Tommy's gone, what shall I do?
5. Tommy fought at Tráfalgár.
Oh, Tommy fought at Trafalgar.
 6. The old Vic to

ry

led the way.
 The brave old Victo

ry

led the way.
7. Tommy's gone for evermore.
Oh, Tommy's gone for evermore.
 [Pg 52]

25. Whisky Johnny.

(HALLIARDS.)

[Listen]

[Pg 53]

1. Oh whisky is the life of man.
Whiskey Johnny.
Oh whisky is the life of man.
Whisky for my Johnny.
 2. Oh whisky makes me pawn my clothes.
And whisky gave me this red nose.
3. Oh whisky killed my poor old dad.
And whisky druv my mother mad.
4. Oh whisky up, and whisky down.
And whisky all around the town.
5. Oh whisky here and whisky there.
It's I'll have whisky everywhere.
6. Oh whisky is the life of man.
It's whisky in an old tin can.
 [Pg 54]

26. Boney was a

warrior.

(HALLIARDS.)

[Listen]

✠ Francois.

1. Boney was a warrior.
Way-ay Yah.
Boney was a warrior.
John France-Wah. [9]
2. Boney beat the Rooshians. (*twice*)
3. Boney beat the Prooshians. (*twice*)
4. Boney went to Möscow. (*twice*)
5. Moscow was a-fire. (*twice*)
6. Boney he came back again. (*twice*)
7. Boney went to Elbow. (*twice*)
8. Boney went to Waterloo. (*twice*)
9. Boney was defeated. (*twice*)
10. Boney was a prisoner
'Board the Billy Ruffian. [10]
11. Boney he was sent away,
'Way to St. Helena.
12. Boney broke his heart, and died. (*twice*)
13. Boney was a warrior. (*twice*)
 [Pg 55]

27. Johnny Boker.

(FORE-SHEET.)

[Listen]

1. Oh do my Johnny Boker,
Come rock and roll me over.
Do my Johnny Boker, do.
2. Oh do my Johnny Boker,

The skipper is a rover.
Do my Johnny, &c.
3. Oh do, &c.
The mate he's never sober.
Do my, &c.
4. Oh do, &c.
The Bo'sun is a tailor.
Do my, &c.
5. Oh do, &c.
 We'll all go on a jam
♪
bo
♪
ree.
♩

Do my, &c.
6. Oh do, &c.
The Packet is a Rollin'.
Do my, &c.
7. Oh do, &c.
We'll pull and haul together.
Do my, &c.
8. Oh do, &c.
We'll haul for better weather.
Do my, &c.
9. Oh do, &c.
 And soon we'll be in Lon
♪
don
♪
 Town.
Do my, &c.
10. Oh do, &c.
Come rock and roll me over.
Do my, &c.
 [Pg 56]

28. Haul away, Joe.

(FORE-SHEET.)

[Listen]

 [Pg 57]

1. Way, haul away, We'll haul away the bowlin'.
Way, haul away, Haul away Joe.
2. Way haul away. The packet is a-rollin'.
3. Way haul away. We'll hang and haul together.
4. Way haul away. We'll haul for better weather.
5. Once
♩
I
♪
had
♩
a
♪
nig
♩
ger
♪
girl,
♩
and she was fat and lazy.
6. Then
♩
I
♪
had
♩
a
♪
Span
♪
ish
♪
girl, she nearly druv me crazy.
7. Geor
♩
die
♪
Charl
♩
ton
♩
had
♪

a pig, and it was double jointed.

8. He took it to the blacksmith's shop to get its trotters pointed.

9. King Louis was the king o' France before the Revolution.

10. King Louis got his head cut off, and spoiled his Constitution.

11. Oh when I was a little boy and so my mother told me.

12. That if I didn't kiss the girls my lips would all go mouldy.

13. Oh once I had a scolding wife, she wasn't very civil.

14. I clapped a plaster on her mouth and sent her to the divvle.

[Pg 58]

29. We'll haul the bowlin'.

(FORE-SHEET.)

[Listen]

† The last word ("haul") of the chorus is not sung but shouted *staccato*.

1. We'll haul the bowlin' so early in the morning.
We'll haul the bowlin', the bowlin' haul! [11]
2. We'll haul the bowlin' for Kitty is my darlin'.
3. We'll haul the bowlin'; the fore-to-gallant bowlin'.
4. We'll haul the bowlin', the skipper is a growlin'.
5. We'll haul the bowlin', the packet is a rollin'.
6. We'll haul the bowlin' so early in the morning.

[Pg 59]

30. Paddy Doyle's boots.

(BUNT SHANTY.)

[Listen]

1. To my way-ay-ay-ah,
We'll pay Paddy Doyle for his boots.
Alternative verses.
2. We'll all throw dirt at the cook.
3. We'll all drink brandy and gin.

FOOTNOTES

[1] i.e. Barbadian, to wit, a native

of Barbados.

[2] The small notes in the piano part are to be played when there is no violin.

[3] This verse was sometimes sung:—
"Now where have you been gone so long
You Yankee Jack wid de sea boots on?"

[4] meal.

[5] Pronounced "Chee-lee men."

[6] Northumbrian equivalent of "so nicely" or "so gently."

[7] Of Australia.

[8] i.e. 35 lashes.

[9] Francois.

[10] Sailor pronunciation of "Bellerophon."

[11] The last word ("haul") of the chorus is not sung but shouted *staccato*.